Parker Ranch

Text by George Engebretson

Richard Kaleioku Palmer Smart
May 21, 1913 — November 12, 1992

This book is dedicated in loving memory to Richard Smart, the last heir of John Palmer Parker I to run the ranch that bears his family name, the Parker Ranch of Hawaii. "The Boss," as he was fondly known, left a legacy of kindness, compassion, and responsible stewardship that will be felt by the people of Kamuela and the island of Hawaii for generations to come.

Front Flap: Lehua blossom of the Ohia tree, part of the varied and exotic flora of the Parker Ranch. Inside front cover and page 1: Parker Ranch landscape, a view of Mauna Kea from the Puuhihale Corral. Below: The P–2 brand denotes Parker, branded in 1992. Opposite page: Branding in Kohala division. Retired foreman, Joe Pacheco. Following pages 6–7: A rainbow promises good luck in the ranch lands near Waikoloa. Paniolos Martin Purdy and Jiro Yamaguchi on horseback on south Kohala coast's Anaehoomalu Beach some years ago.

Copyright 1993 by the Parker Ranch. Produced for the Parker Ranch by Legacy Publishing, Carpinteria, CA.

Project Manager/Editor: Sheila M. Cantillon
Design: J. Schultz
Production: Nancy M. Swanson

Photography by Alfredo Furelos,
with supplementary photographs
by Reggie David, Rana Productions
and from the Parker Ranch
Archives.

Hawaiian language/Paniolo termi-
nology glossary by Robert Hind III,
livestock manager, Parker Ranch,
and Sonny Keakealani, livestock
foreman, Parker Ranch.

Printed in Thailand
ISBN 1-56933-005-0

CONTENTS

Hawaii's Cattle Kingdom

Across the mountain's great flank he rides, his horse surefooted in the rocky scrub. Swaddled against the brittle chill, hat pulled low over a face of pure rawhide, he is the classic figure of the American West.

Yet there's something different about this familiar scene. For this is the West with a tropical twist, and a cowboy unlike any other. His wide-brimmed hat sports a garland of *ilima* blossoms and tiny ferns, his dust-caked shirt a Polynesian print, his weathered features a mix of Europe, Asia and the South Pacific. His mountain is Mauna Kea, one of the world's highest volcanoes. His horizon is the deep, equatorial sea stretching away to the west.

He is a *paniolo*, a Hawaiian cowboy, and his world is Parker Ranch—Hawaii's magnificent cattle kingdom. A world of sparkling days and brisk, star-sprinkled nights. Of historical drama and the big business that is modern ranching. Of spectacular beauty and just plain hard work.

It's a big, brawny land under a wide open sky—in an island community where land is more precious than gold. Parker Ranch, in fact, is the third-largest spread in

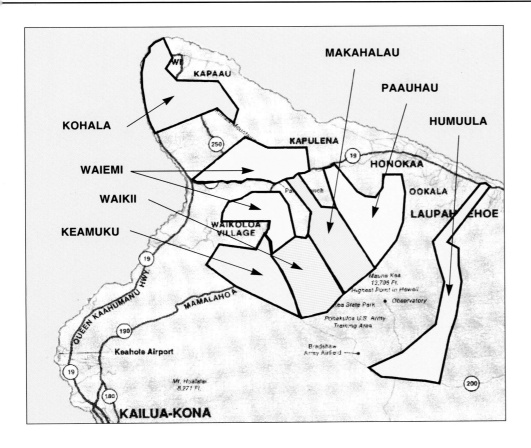

Preceding pages 8–9: Mamane tree on the slopes of Mauna Kea. Opposite page, clockwise from the top: Paniolos riding home after a long day. A wild rose. Weaned calves. Above right: In the Mana division of the ranch, at 4,000 feet elevation. This is below the original site of Mana Hale, the first Parker home. Above: The modern Parker Ranch encompasses 210,000 acres, including four major divisions; the Kohala to the north, the Mauna Kea to the southwest, the Mana to the northeast, and the Keamuku/Humuula to the south.

the U.S., its 225,000 acres spilling over sea cliffs and sweeping across stark volcanic range. Its 55,000 cattle graze both in mountain mists and in pastures overlooking powder-white beaches.

But at Parker Ranch, *big* is only the beginning.

It is, for one thing, history in the making. Today's Ranch is the latest chapter in a powerful saga—one surpassing the imagination of any frontier novelist. The story of the Ranch is one of incredible tragedy and dreams fulfilled, of cattle barons and colorful rogues. A young sailor jumps ship, befriends a king and builds an empire. A beautiful princess disappears into a churning sea after her young husband's untimely death. *A bon vivant* friend of the rich and powerful lights his cigars with dollar bills as Ranch fortunes drop into the red. An heir-apparent postpones his birthright to make his mark as a leading man on Broadway. If it hadn't actually happened, no one would believe it.

More than just big, Parker Ranch is a thriving business, with profitable cattle operations, real estate dealings that shape the island's future, and visitor attractions that are among the most fascinating in the fiftieth state. Using state-of-the-art technology this mid-Pacific ranch keeps a mix of Angus, Brangus and Hereford cattle yielding over ten million pounds of beef annually for U.S. and Canadian markets.

More than just big, Parker Ranch has been a way of life for generations of island people. When Ranch folks gather under the great Puuopelu pine at Christmas or throng the corrals at Paniolo Park on the Fourth of July, they are a true rainbow of races and faces—a tropical blend of ethnic diversity. From Japan and Portugal, from California and New England, their parents and grandparents came to work the pastures and paddocks of Parker Ranch.

For more than a century, the Ranch has claimed a hefty chunk of

11

The annual 4th of July horse races and rodeo. Opposite page, top to bottom: Francis Shim, paniolo. Godfrey Kainoa, foreman for Keamuku section. Mark Yamaguchi, paniolo.

the Island of Hawaii, the one that gave the entire archipelago its name. Kamehameha, the warrior king who unified the islands and bestowed this name, figures prominently in the story of Parker Ranch.

Today Hawaii is called simply the Big Island; all the other islands in the chain could easily fit within its palm-lined shores. Larger than Connecticut, it includes nearly every environment imaginable, from rain forest to desert, from teeming coral reefs to snow-shrouded mountain peaks. Here are ancient *heiau* (temples), broad carpets of waving sugar cane, tiny beach hamlets and world-famous marlin fishing grounds.

Parker Ranch is headquartered in the cowtown of Kamuela, an upcountry village slung in the saddle of two great mountains. It's an emerald setting defined by rustic homes, rolling pasture land and gently sculpted foothills. Here, the tropical sun eases the chill at

twenty-five hundred feet above sea level, and fine, light mists drift in curtains from the east.

From Kamuela, also called Waimea, Parker Ranch spreads out in every direction. It rises up the rugged slopes of 13,796-foot Mauna Kea, where the Ranch's nineteenth-century patriarch once hunted wild steer with his arsenal of muskets. It dips down into lush valleys where old Hawaiians worked the land and fished the sea. It runs out across glistening fields of lava to the sea, where sumptuous resorts and golf courses have been carved out of solid rock. And it spreads over some of the finest grazing land on earth—cooled by tradewinds and carpeted with rye, clover and African Kikuyu grass.

For the *malihini* (newcomer), Parker Ranch is another version of the Aloha State—the flip side of beach luaus and mai tais. Visitors can discover Hawaii's cattle country in a variety of ways—by

12

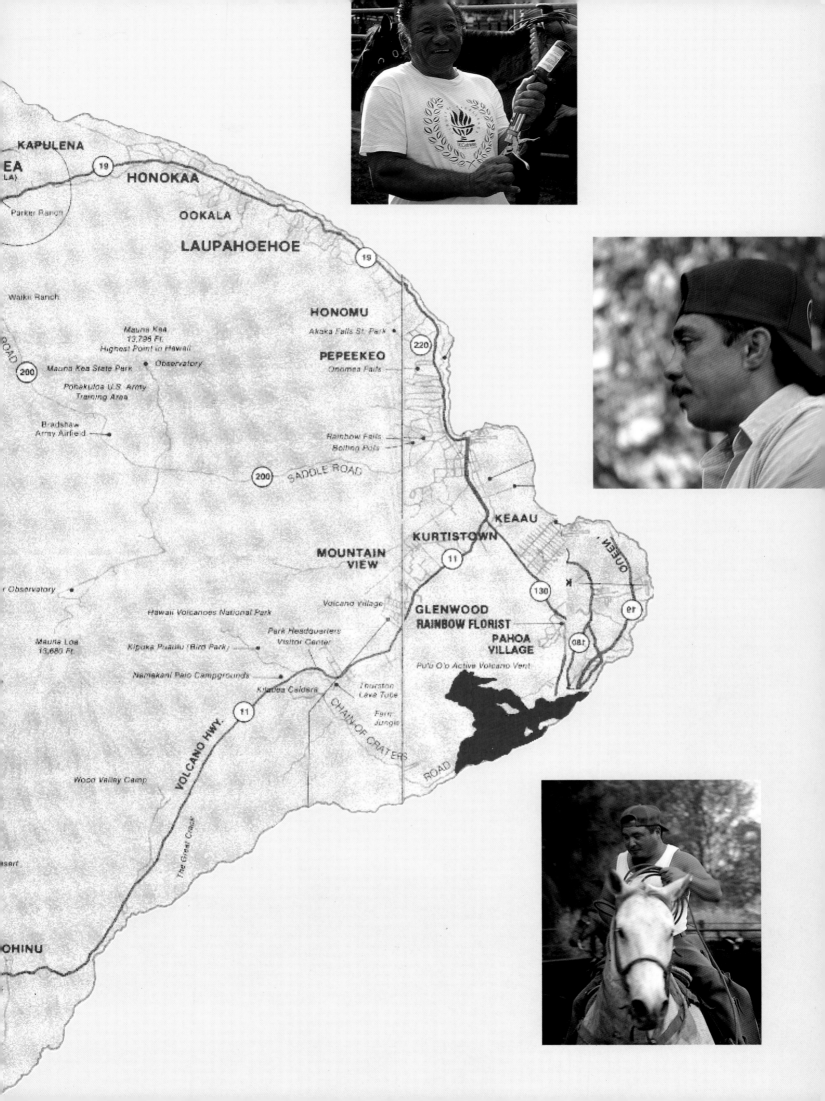

Opposite page, left to right: A wild poppy. Monarch butterfly. Wild feral pigs. Kahili Ginger. Below: A typically beautiful sunrise in Humuula. Right: Pueo, a Hawaiian owl. Parker Ranch has a wide range of fauna.

car, on foot or on horseback. They can four-wheel-drive into the outback, hike the pristine pastures or ride the range on the trail of the paniolo. Or they can stroll through charming Kamuela, a completely Hawaiian town, but one where the merchants peddle cowboy hats, tack and wood-burning stoves.

In Kamuela, they can immerse themselves at the Parker Ranch Visitor Center, with a multi-media presentation and a museum brimming with historic photos and documents, with the art and artifacts of the area's colorful past. Here are priceless memorabilia, charts of genealogy and crude nineteenth-century veterinary tools. Or they can visit the sprawling estate at Puuopelu, where the Parkers' early ancestral home now stands next to the residence of the last Ranch owner Richard Smart. Mana was built in the mid-1800s, and appears from the outside to be a basic New England-style home, but it is built

completely of the unusual Hawaiian koa wood. Here more of the history of the Parker family and the region can be viewed through photographs and letters, while the visitor admires the tropical richness of the wood interior. At Puuopelu, the luxurious furnishings and excellent Impressionist art collection are a memorable attraction in their own right.

Together, these two beautiful homes tell the story of Parker Ranch. One represents the Ranch today—a thriving cattle operation, a leader in the industry. The other embodies the frontier spirit of the early years, when a footloose New Englander named John Parker first laid eyes on this magnificent land.

15

CHAPTER I

The Parker Ranch Saga

The King's Gift

John Palmer Parker liked what he saw. After his many months at sea, from New England around the Horn, any landfall was a welcome sight. But this was unlike anything the stocky nineteen-year-old had ever seen: a lush, palm-picketed shoreline flanked by a gentle sea and dotted with sleepy thatched villages. Above the coast rose broad reaches of stark lava rock and grassy plains, sweeping up the high flanks of majestic volcanoes.

The year was 1809, just a single generation after white men had first encountered these tropical isles–named the Sandwich Islands by British explorer Captain James Cook. Though a few westerners had settled along the archipelago, most stayed only long enough to take on food and water and to trade for the valuable sandalwood harvested from island forests. Parker's own vessel was a trader seeking sandalwood on this island of Hawaii, home of the fabled King Kamehameha, who had brought the islands together under single rule.

Ashore the next morning at the crude harbor of Kawaihae, John Parker watched the native work parties dragging great logs down from the windswept highlands. The forests, he saw, were already showing signs of depletion, as demand skyrocketed and more and more of the fragrant wood was shipped off to the Orient to be carved into furniture and made into incense.

The son of an enterprising Massachusetts shipowner, John Parker sniffed opportunity along this sweeping leeward shore. Born in Newton, Massachusetts, a descendant of New England founding fathers, he had taken a keen interest in the world of commerce—excelling in mathematics at Framingham Academy, keeping the books for the family business, and eventually signing on with the merchant ship as captain's clerk. But young John also knew a thing or two about grueling manual labor. On the

family homestead at Newton, he had taken a hand in planting, harvesting, animal husbandry and many other tedious chores. Aboard ship, he had learned the rigors of sailing the high seas.

What would fuel the island's fragile economy, he wondered, when the precious sandalwood was gone? During his brief visits ashore, he learned of the thousands of maverick cattle that roamed Hawaii's remote plains and valleys. These rangy beasts were the legacy of British Captain George Vancouver, who had presented Kamehameha with the first five head only sixteen years earlier. In his inquiries, Parker also discovered that a small number of foreigners had actually settled on the island. A fortunate few had even won positions of influence with the warrior king.

John Parker was captivated–with the intense tropical beauty, with the gentle natives, with the scent of opportunity. And when his skipper weighed anchor for Asia–his sandalwood cargo far lighter than he'd hoped–he sailed without the clerk Parker. For young John had jumped ship, hiding in a thicket until the merchant vessel dropped below the horizon. It was a bold move for any nineteen-year-old five thousand miles from home. For John Palmer Parker, it was also a long first step toward building one of the largest cattle ranches in the world.

In the days and weeks that followed, Parker set to work learning the lay of the land. He befriended the natives in the area, who helped him build a small hale

19

Preceding pages 16–17: John Palmer Parker I (inset); early view of Kealakekua, Hawaii, by John Webber. Opposite page: an early map of the Hawaiian Islands. Above: lava stone lamps, of the type used by the Hawaiians at the time Parker landed.

Venton October 9 1817

my Dear John Improve this opertunety of writing to you
and Sending it by the messinors which is a grate Sadisfaction
to me that your are like to have the Gospel of Christ amongst
you my anciety for your Soul has been Grater than for your Boda
which has many times caused me to cry Lord have mercy on the
immortal Part I hope you will receive them and do everething
your Power in Promoting the Gospel God Give you Grace to live
godly life that if we never See oneanother in this world we may m
together in the Kingdom of heaven which is my humble Prayers for
and all my Children —

I received your letter dated February 13 1817 and have not hard fro
you Sence the time Seems long my Dear Child — and when I read the lett
it over come me So much that I was not able to Speak for I than was lotte
on your Return home your letters was wet with tears —
I have wrote twice Sence to you and Sent you a Chest to the care of Mr Pilm
hope you have got it containing those articles three Coats two wescoats two
three Shirters three hankerchifs one Large Silver Spoon one bible one Lar
volem of Mr Flavel works and other Books and Some artikles i dont
my Dear Dear John if it was Consistent with the will of heaven that I wa
See your Face once more but not my will but thine be done o God wh
rules in heaven and amongst the Children of men —
your Father is well and my health is as Good as I can expect Poor
Patience has been confined to hir Bead 8 months your Brother Wife
and Sister was well three weaks ago John Pidgon was home this Sum
and is a very Prosspers Gong nan Samuel went a voige to Sea and
never have hard from him we expect he is loft

All Friends continues theair love and Good wishes for you

Mr John P Parker   From your Aged Mother
                        whose Sincear Prayers is that you may Sarve G
                        in Spirit and torith with my best to you during
                        my Life Ann Parker

Opposite page: a 1814 letter to John Palmer Parker from his mother, Ann Parker. Right: King Kamehameha I.

(house) and plant the ground around it. He studied the rudiments of their melodious Polynesian tongue and explored the rugged coastline. In short order, the industrious haole (foreigner) came to the attention of Kamehameha, who held court at Kealakekua.

When the king sent for him, Parker impressed Kamehameha–a monarch still wary of white men–with his energy and vision. And so he was offered a job as manager of the royal fish ponds at nearby Honaunau. For nearly two years he performed this duty with distinction, currying favor with both king and commoners. But in 1811, Parker's dream of tapping the island's promise took a detour. The thrill of the high seas was still in his blood, and when another merchant ship called at the Big Island just after his twenty-first birthday–bound for the Orient–he signed on for one more adventure.

In Canton, the ship's crew found the War of 1812 in full vigor–and all shipping halted by a British blockade. And so they languished for nearly two years, harbor-bound in China. When at last the vessel made port at Kawaihae in 1815, Parker was a seasoned twenty-five-year-old more determined than ever to leave his imprint on the Sandwich Islands. His first hurdle, of course, was ingratiating himself with Kamehameha all over again. But after some discussion, the sturdy

Above: Ebenezer Parker. Opposite page: King Kamehameha III; Parker Ranch land with the Mauna Kea in the background, as it might have looked to John Parker I.

haole convinced the king he was back to stay.

He also showed Kamehameha his new, state-of-the-art American musket and, before long, found himself the first man allowed to shoot the herds of cattle that roamed the countryside. Their beef, tallow and hides were invaluable in bartering for other goods. What's more, he was granted a small parcel in the Hamakua district and immediately set about digging irrigation ditches and planting taro and garden vegetables. Soon he was supplying both islanders and visiting ships with these sought-after commodities.

The following year, John Parker married Kipikane, the daughter of a high-ranking chief. In 1819, Kipikane, who took the Christian name Rachel, bore him a daughter, Mary Ann. Eight years later, there was a son, John Palmer Parker II, and two years after that, another named Ebenezer. It was the beginning of an island dynasty that would span the next two centuries.

By then, the New England transplant had forged a place for himself as Hawaii's most prolific hunter of wild cattle, or pipi. Due mostly to his efforts, salt beef was replacing sandalwood as the island's chief product, and the Parkers were spending much of their time in the highland village of Waimea, deep in the heart of cattle country. So great was the demand

and so thick and dangerous were the ranging herds that the current monarch, Kamehameha III, sent to California for Spanish-Mexican vaqueros to help work the ranges. These colorful cowboys, with their upturned sombreros, ornate saddles and flashing spurs, were known to the natives as paniolo, for Espanol.

In the years that followed, as more and more foreigners sought their fortunes in the area, Waimea became a bustling center of trade. As Parker's family grew, he made the permanent move to town, running a small store and building his own herd of domesticated cattle. The wild, ranging pipi were now greatly reduced in numbers—even protected by royal decree–and most of the old hunters had moved on to other pursuits. Changing with the times, Parker leased acreage on the northern slope of Mauna Kea to graze and run his animals.

By late 1845, John Parker's vision was undimmed. Now a ruddy, white-bearded rancher of fifty-five, he eyed his leased parcel and resolved to build a permanent ranch there. He and Rachel walked the land and selected a beautiful homesite twelve miles southeast of Waimea town. After petitioning the king's Land Commission, they waited more than a year and were at last granted two acres of land, a virtual gift from Kamehameha III for the token payment of just ten dollars. It was January 8, 1847.

On this dramatic site overlooking the broad plains of Waimea and the Kohala mountains beyond, the Parkers built their showplace home, Mana Hale. Over the years, Mana Hale would become the nerve center of the Parker Ranch, which would soon

Building a Dynasty

take its place as a major force in the fast-changing Hawaiian Islands.

The winds of change were blowing briskly across the highlands of Waimea. A year after receiving his first two acres, Parker bought another 640 acres surrounding Mana. A few months later, he purchased another thousand. The price: seventy-five cents an acre. At last, he had sufficient land to graze and raise his growing herd. He also began raising sheep, turkeys and chickens, and planted a cornucopia of crops in and around Mana. With its neat corrals, bustling dairy, meat storage house and servants' quarters, the new homestead soon became a popular way-station for cross-island travelers. With his generous hospitality and knack for spinning a good story, John Parker cemented his position as one of Hawaii's most influential men.

His two sons, meanwhile, were preparing to carry forward the budding Parker legacy. John II, the amiable first-born, soon married a beautiful full-Hawaiian girl named Hanai. Because Hanai was kauwa, of the island slave caste, their union met

with much disapproval, especially from the royal-born Rachel Kipikane. Several of the native kupuna even predicted that no child of such a marriage would survive. But John II and Hanai moved into a second koa house which old John built for them at Mana, and built a strong and lasting marriage—even after the native prediction came true and their only child, Samuel, died shortly after birth.

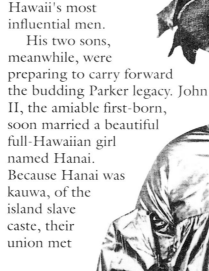

For his part, second son Ebenezer grew into a tall, handsome young man with the regal bearing of the alii (monarchy). After establishing an island-wide reputation as a ladies' man, Eben wooed and won the enchanting Kilia, a maiden of storied beauty. A native of Kohala, Kilia was on Maui when he found her, pledged to marry a high chief of that island. Equally smitten, however, she sailed to Hawaii after Eben's return, where the two were married and welcomed with open arms by the Parkers of Mana. Over the next few years, the striking couple was blessed with four children: Mary, Ebenezer II, Nancy and Samuel, the boy who would figure prominently in the future of Parker Ranch.

But when Eben was still a young man, tragedy struck. In March 1855, while eating plover, he swallowed a small bone that worked its way into his intestines, killing him at the age of twenty-six. Kilia was consumed with grief–wearing Eben's undershirt for months after his death and

sleeping in a tent she ordered pitched for her at the windswept family cemetery at Mana.

Nursed back to health by her in-laws, Kilia eventually remarried for a short time. But at the age of twenty-seven, a year after her first-born, ten-year-old son Ebenezer II, had died, she longed to return to Maui. In early 1861 she set sail by outrigger canoe across the treacherous Alenuihaha Channel. Within sight of the send-off party, the canoe and its passengers were swamped by great swells, quickly pulled under and never seen again.

Seven years later, old John Palmer Parker died. His passing marked the end of an era, and of an epic fifty-nine-year career in the Hawaiian Islands. Most of the Ranch holdings were divided

Opposite page: Kilia Parker. Above: Samuel Parker.

equally between his sole surviving son, John II, and Ebenezer's only living son Sam. It was a considerable estate, for John II had been quietly building upon his father's foundation. Working slowly but surely, father and son had added Ranch acreage–buying one hundred and fifty acres here, four hundred acres there

In personal style and management philosophy, the two heirs were as different as night and day. John II continued to live the simple life at Mana, eventually buying a new homestead called Puuopelu in 1879 and moving Ranch operations to the town of Waimea. Sam, on the other hand, was athletic, flamboyant–and as tall and handsome as his father had

been. In the years to come, this colorful character would place Mana indelibly on the island social map, creating a mecca for royalty, adventurers and dignitaries from all over the world.

While attending Oahu College in Honolulu, Sam created his first big stir. His affair with the noble-born young socialite Harriet Panana Napela resulted in a child born out of wedlock who was sent by Panana's mother to an orphanage. Shortly afterward, in 1871, Sam married Panana and brought her to Mana. The dashing couple set the tone early on, when Hawaii's king and queen arrived as two of their very first guests. Sam immediately set about adding creature comforts to the old homestead–remodeling a cottage into a posh guest house, sprucing up the gardens, rebuilding the horse pen and relocating some of the outbuildings further from Mana Hale.

Over the next three decades, the couple bore nine children and

Opposite page, left: King David Kalakaua (seated), Samuel Parker (reclining), and Jack Low; right: Harriet Panana Parker Above, upper: John Palmer Parker II; lower: Samuel Parker (left) and King Kalakaua (right) seated in the King's office.

became the very hub of society in the region. The level of pomp and entertainment at Mana rivaled even that staged by Sam's old classmate, David Kalakaua. Now Hawaii's king, Kalakaua and his queen, Kapiolani, were bent on reviving the long-dormant Hawaiian culture–in music, in sports, in the traditional arts. Kindred souls, Sam and the King spent considerable time in each other's company. Parker became a fixture at Iolani Palace in Honolulu and was even named a lifetime member of the King's House of Nobles, with the honorary title of colonel. In Waimea, the affable, generous Colonel Sam was so popular that the town was renamed in his honor: Kamuela, the Hawaiian word for Samuel.

But this lavish lifestyle was also starting to drain the Ranch coffers. Sam Parker was neither a cattleman nor a businessman, and the job of tending the growing acreage and some five thousand head of cattle

fell to his industrious uncle John II. Unfortunately, John wasn't the dynamic leader his father had been, and he found himself unable to counter the effects of Colonel Sam's spendthrift ways. The Ranch's failing financial state drove a sharp wedge between the two Parkers, despite the fact that John and Hanai had recently adopted Sam's oldest son–John Palmer Parker III.

The situation grew even worse during Sam's ill-starred venture into sugar cane. Despite his uncle's warnings, he was determined to try his hand at this lucrative new crop, which was burgeoning throughout the Hawaiian kingdom. But his new plantation was a failure from the start, and Colonel Sam found himself heavily in debt to sugar baron Claus Spreckels, his partner in the venture.

Unable to liquidate the debt, the Parkers were forced to mortgage the Ranch, which was placed in a trust in 1887. For the first time in its history, the spread was outside the direct control of family members. The move began a long reign by several outside managers, and precipitated the rapid physical decline of old John Parker II. He passed away in late 1891 at Sam Parker's Honolulu residence, leaving his half of the Ranch to his adopted son John III. The funeral in Honolulu was a grand event, attended by Queen Liliuokalani–sister of the late David Kalakaua, Princes Kawananakoa and Jonah Kuhio Kalanianaole, Governor Archibald Cleghorn and myriad friends and relatives. Because John II had also been a life member of the House of Nobles, all government flags flew at half-mast. John Palmer Parker II was laid to rest at the family plot at Mana.

The youngest John Parker was already sixteen when his granduncle–his adopted father–died. Two years later, he married a bright, assertive woman three years his senior; the pair had been introduced by Liliuokalani herself at a party at Iolani Palace. She was Elizabeth Jane Lanakila Dowsett, daughter of wealthy Honolulu businessman James Dowsett. Though none could

Above: John Palmer Parker III. Opposite page: Annie Thelma Kahiluonapuaapiilani Parker.

know it at the time, the doughty Elizabeth would have considerable effect on the future of Parker Ranch. Less than a year after their marriage, the couple became the parents of a daughter, Annie Thelma Kahiluonapuaapiilani Parker. But two months later, John III was dead of inflammatory rheumatism. And yet another stone marker went up at the family plot at Mana. By Hawaiian law, his half-interest in the Ranch—John II's half—passed directly on to the new baby.

As little Thelma grew into childhood, Elizabeth began the search for a good manager, one who could cure the Ranch's ills while looking after her daughter's interests. The man she found was Alfred Wellington Carter, the respected Honolulu businessman

The Carter Years

and judge whose steady hand would guide Parker Ranch for nearly a half-century. With vision and financial acumen, Carter would do more to advance its fortunes than anyone but old John Palmer Parker himself.

Alfred Carter was a keiki o ka aina, a child of the land. Born in Honolulu in 1867, this son of a whaler had graduated summa cum laude from Yale Law School and distinguished himself in various positions in island commerce and government. A sturdy, sincere, forthright man, he had been enamored of Waimea since the age of nineteen, when he visited Sam and Panana at Mana. Now, on the threshold of a new century, he quickly won the confidence of both Elizabeth and Colonel Sam.

The deal was struck in September 1899, when Carter was appointed the legal guardian of Annie Thelma Parker as well as trustee-manager of her property. Under this agreement, he would also manage Sam's half-interest in the Ranch. Carter sailed to

Kawaihae in January 1900 and was dismayed, though not discouraged, by what he found. The rangy herd needed serious upgrading, and many cattle ran wild on the inaccessible slopes of Mauna Kea. During regular periods of drought, he was told, thousands of them died from inadequate water supply. Pasture land appeared unproductive, often overgrazed.

The Ranch now sprawled over some 300,000 acres, but only 20,000 or so were fenced in. Consequently, many of the cattle wandered off into the hands of part-time rustlers or hungry islanders. What's more, most of this vast acreage was leased from other landowners, and many of the leases were due to terminate in only a few years.

And so Alfred Carter set to work. Marketing was an initial concern; Parker Ranch beef,

30

though substandard, was still going to market. Carter suspended the sale of cattle while he expanded facilities for fattening. This involved both building new paddocks and laying pipeline to bring water down from the Kohala Mountains to the best grasslands. Elsewhere, he installed new fencing, set up cattle scales and restocked hay storage facilities. He began upgrading the herd with pure, pedigreed bulls and heifers, carefully selected and imported from the finest cattle ranches in America. Perhaps most important, he turned his attention to those nearly expired leases–offering to buy the parcels even in the face of opposition from old Colonel Sam.

Once the honeymoon period was over, in fact, Sam Parker was proving to be one of Carter's biggest hurdles. Now a widower, the middle-aged bon vivant resented the funneling of revenues back into operations. Any reduction in his personal income–even for the brighter future of the Ranch–was met with great bluster and resistance. Finally weary of butting heads with the intractable Carter, Sam offered to sell his half-interest to Thelma's trust. He was offered six hundred thousand dollars.

But then Sam Parker decided he wanted it all–lock, stock and barrel. And so began one of the most dramatic episodes in the history of Parker Ranch. In the spring of

31

Opposite page: Alfred Wellington Carter. Above: water towers which are part of the irrigation system that was one of Carter's accomplishments at the Ranch.

1904, Alfred Carter was in Honolulu on business when word came that Sam planned to take the ranch by force. Carter was on the next steamship to Kawaihae. When he arrived at Waimea, he learned that a group of armed Parker loyalists were camped in the eastern Hamakua region, awaiting orders. He was confronted by the one-handed Eben Low, a Parker cousin with a reputation for gunplay.

With two pistols strapped to his hips, Low stormed into the manager's office and informed him that he was taking possession of the ranch on behalf of Sam Parker. Carter refused to budge and promised to meet force with force. When Eben Low stalked out–threatening to blow up the office with dynamite–Carter then took to horse and found the group of paniolo (cowboys) camped in the Hamakua bush. He asked them to choose sides then and there. Though some of the cowboys were related to Colonel Sam, they all vowed their allegiance to Carter.

He then rode to Kona to file a countersuit against Sam, who had sued for control of the Ranch and for the revocation of Thelma's guardianship. What followed was two-and-a-half years of snarling litigation, with the Ranch in receivership awaiting the outcome. After the case had stretched all the way to the U.S. Supreme Court, Sam Parker threw in the towel. In a dramatic about-face, he offered to settle out of court by selling his share to Thelma's trust–after much dickering, for the original offer of six hundred thousand dollars. At last, in September 1906, the Ranch became the sole property of Annie Thelma Parker, who was then twelve years old and living with her mother in San Francisco.

In the following years, Alfred Carter renewed his efforts to make Parker Ranch profitable–this time without family obstacles. Puffing on his ever-present cigar, he worked tirelessly, always with great consideration for his paniolos and other employees, who had proved their loyalty during the takeover attempt.

He continued to upgrade the stock, vowing to build a Hereford herd unequalled anywhere. He brought in the very best thoroughbred stallions from mainland ranches. He imported hearty new grasses from all over the world–cocksfoot and Yorkshire fog from England, Rhodes grass from South Africa, bluegrass from Kentucky. He bought tens of thousands of acres in fee simple. He began a major sheep station on Mauna Kea, exporting the wool. He fenced the range. And in 1909, Carter established the Hawaii Meat Company, a co-op of seven Big Island ranches. With a new feedlot outside Honolulu, island cattle could now be shipped to Oahu for fattening and slaughter under the ranchers' own terms.

He also kept an eye out for Thelma, whom he had come to love as his own daughter. She and Elizabeth–whom everyone called Aunt Tootsie–often traveled from San Francisco to stay, and Carter took special care to familiarize her with the Ranch. Unlike Colonel Sam, Aunt Tootsie saw eye-to-eye with her manager on operations. Together, they guided Parker Ranch to the top of the industry–a

Opposite page, left: Thelma Parker Smart holding her son, Richard Palmer Kaleioku Smart; right: Henry Gaillard Smart. Above: Elizabeth "Aunt Tootsie" Dowsett Parker (second from left) with Richard Smart (center), in a riding party at the Parker Ranch.

spread greatly admired by the cattlemen who visited from all over the country.

In 1912, as mother and daughter were returning from San Francisco for the summer, the striking part-Hawaiian girl met a dashing young Virginian named Henry Gaillard Smart. The shipboard romance grew serious and only three weeks later the couple married. The following year, the people of Parker Ranch celebrated a grand event in any dynasty–the birth of a male heir. The proud new parents named him Richard Palmer Kaleioku Smart and before he was a year old, took him off to tour Europe.

When Thelma was seventeen, she and Aunt Tootsie had been invited to the coronation of George V in London. The wide-eyed girl had marveled at the pomp and history she discovered there and on the Continent, and she was determined to share it all with her new family. Overriding her mother's objections, they sailed for France in early 1914–despite the new baby, despite the second one on the way, despite the specter of war that shrouded all of Europe.

And then tragedy struck, over and over again. Thelma fell ill upon their arrival in Paris, and when her second child, Elizabeth Ella, was born, she was sickly as well. To make matters worse, the

33

Germans attacked in August, and the ailing family fled Paris in one of the last motorcars out of Paris before it was closed under siege. In LeHavre, the Smarts boarded a steamship for New York, where the frail Elizabeth Ella died at the Plaza Hotel. Henry took his family to his parents' summer home in Virginia Beach, where Thelma's illness was diagnosed as tuberculosis.

Enter Aunt Tootsie, who arrived from San Francisco to take the Smarts back to the Islands. The homecoming was not to be. In California, Thelma died in Aunt Tootsie's home, as Hawaiian musicians from the 1914 San Francisco Exposition serenaded her from the street below. She was twenty years old. Eleven months later, Gaillard Smart–despondent and stricken with meningitis–died in Virginia. All that remained of the promising young family was the toddler Richard, not yet three years old and the sole heir to the entire Parker Ranch.

Aunt Tootsie won custody of Richard and raised her only grandchild in the Parker tradition of dedication and responsibility. The heir-apparent grew up in the San Francisco Bay Area, making annual summer visits to the Ranch with his grandmother. Alfred Carter, still grieving over his beloved Thelma, took the boy under his wing and showed him the ropes of Parker Ranch. It was an education that would continue halfway through the twentieth century.

At the same time, Carter was building upon past successes. Over the next two decades, the Ranch continued to grow, at one point passing the half-million-acre mark, more than half the size of Rhode Island. Its purebred herd of 30,000 Herefords supplied many other ranches with breeding stock. The Oahu feedlot was expanded. Carter hired ambitious immigrants–Japanese, Portuguese, Chinese–as paniolos and other workers, becoming one of Hawaii's first equal opportunity employers.

In the meantime, Richard Smart was learning a very different craft. He had loved the theatre from an early age and upon graduation from high school, enrolled in the acting program at the Pasadena Playhouse. On his twentieth

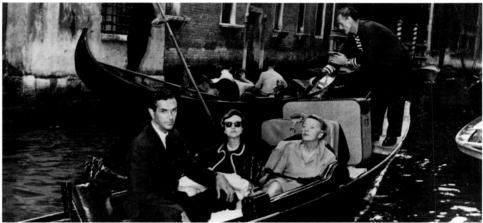

birthday in 1933, Smart became the sole owner of Parker Ranch. But with the sixty-six-year-old Alfred Carter in firm control of the Ranch's fortunes, he was able to begin pursuing a career on the stage.

For nearly thirty years, he earned rave reviews on Broadway and in top cabarets in the U.S. and abroad. As a leading man, he starred opposite Nanette Fabray in "Bloomer Girl," Eve Arden in "Two for the Show," Carol Channing in "Wonderful Town" and in dozens of other plays and musicals, working with the likes of Charlie Chaplin, Betty Hutton, Mary Martin and Keenan Wynn. As a member in good standing of cafe society, he headlined such clubs as the Coconut Grove in Los Angeles, the Monte Carlo in New York and the Lido in Paris.

In 1936 he married the actress Patricia Havens-Monteagle and the couple had two sons, Tony and Gilliard, born in 1937 and 1940, respectively. All the while, Smart kept in close contact with the

Ranch, making annual visits to meet with and learn from Alfred Carter. Even after Carter retired in 1937, the old cattleman continued to guide the operation in tandem with his son, Hartwell, who took the helm as manager and remained for twenty-three years.

During World War II, Parker Ranch made significant contributions to the war effort, as a

35

Opposite page: Richard Smart in a publicity photo for "Bloomer Girl," 1947–1948. Above: Richard Smart with (clockwise from top): Keenan Wynn and Brenda Forbes in "Two for the Show"; friends Margaret Lindsay and Dorothy Mackaill, sightseeing in Venice; Kathryn Kimber in "Two for the Show"; Nanette Fabray in "Bloomer Girl," 1947–1948.

John Palmer Parker
1790 - 1868

Ebenezer Parker
1829 - 1855

John Palmer Parker II
1827 - 1891

Samuel Parker
1852 - 1920

John Palmer Parker III
1875 - 1894

Thelma Parker Smart
1894 - 1914

Richard Palmer Smart
1913 - ....

PARKER FAMILY TREE
Showing ownership through six generations

The Parker family tree (from top and from left to right): John Palmer Parker I (1790–1868); Ebenezer Parker (1829–1855); John Palmer Parker II (1827–1891); Samuel Parker (1852–1920); John Palmer Parker III (1875–1894); Thelma Parker Smart (1894–1914); Richard Palmer Smart (1913–1992).

training ground for soldiers and Marines. More than fifty thousand servicemen trained on as many acres, an area dubbed "Camp Tarawa" by survivors of that bloody Pacific battle. Also during the war, Aunt Tootsie died in Los Angeles at the age of seventy-one. The trust of Annie Thelma Parker expired at her death, and the Ranch officially became the property of Richard Smart.

In April of 1949, Alfred Wellington Carter passed away–an eighty-two-year-old ranching legend. And in 1960, Richard Smart came home to stay, trading his Manhattan penthouse for the family home at Puuopelu. After an intense learning period–huddling with the Ranch's cattlemen, lawyers and accountants–Smart began improvements which would make Parker Ranch the economic power it is today.

He restructured breeding management, expanded irrigation facilities and experimented with feed supplements. In the face of tough competition from USDA grade mainland beef, he began a major expansion of the Hawaii Meat Co. feedlot on Oahu. In Kamuela, he spruced up Ranch headquarters and other buildings with a Monarchy-era design called Hawaiian Victorian and eventually built the Parker Ranch Visitor Center, with its museum, restaurant and saddle shop. In

1981, he opened the first-class Kahilu Theatre, named for his mother, with his own performance in "Oh, Coward!"

In addition, he sold or leased out unprofitable coastal acreage for resort use. The first of these developments was the Mauna Kea Beach Hotel, opened in 1964 by Laurence Rockefeller at Kaunaoa Bay. The beautiful crescent beach and the land around it were leased from the Ranch for a period of ninety-nine years. Other developers followed suit–Boise Cascade and Signal Oil among them–and state-of-the-art hotels and golf courses began to appear in the glistening lava fields of the island's lee shore. Today, the Big Island's Kohala Coast is considered one of the world's premier resort destinations.

Smart also instituted many programs to benefit Ranch employees–in education, in health care, in culture and the arts. Like Alfred Carter, he made the Ranch folk his primary concern. Many of them, after all, were descendants of those paniolos who had worked so loyally for John Palmer Parker a century before.

From their point of view, Richard Smart's return was like the last piece of a puzzle falling into place. For the people of Parker Ranch, it was fitting and proper that a Parker had once again taken the reins. Even after his death in 1992, Richard Smart has taken care of the Ranch by leaving it in trust for the people of Parker Ranch.

CHAPTER II

The Paniolo

A Proud Tradition

Paniolo: In the beginning it was the Hawaiian word for Espanol, after the first Mexican *vaqueros* imported from California. Over the years, it has come to mean much more.

Paniolo stands for strength. Retired cowboy George Purdy remembers *hoau*–shipping cattle to market by swimming them out to boats offshore, in the days before livestock was loaded from wharves. Mounted on Percheron horses, cowboys muscled the panicky cattle through the surf and lashed them to the side of the longboats for transfer to an inter-island steamer anchored further out.

Preceding pages 38-39: Historic photograph of paniolos on the Parker Ranch. Above: Paniolos Martin Purdy, Giro Yamaguchi and Donnie DeSilva at Anaehoomalu Beach. Right: Corky Bryan, Livestock Marketing Manager in the Waikii section of the Mauna Kea division, driving cattle. Opposite page: Cattle drive.

Paniolo stands for courage. Consider the story of Palaika Lindsey, a turn-of-the-century Ranch cowboy. One day, with manager Alfred Carter, Lindsey was working a belligerent bull in Mauna Kea's remote scrub land. When Carter's horse threw him, breaking his leg and knocking him unconscious, Lindsey hoisted him across his back and trudged five miles over rocky plain and crumbling lava rock to find help.

Paniolo stands for resourcefulness. When the Ranch bought the champion bull Oddfellow, Palaika's brother Johnny was sent to lead the great Hereford back from Hilo. But before long, Oddfellow's huge hoofs became painfully gashed and bloodied on the tough lava terrain, nearly crippling the prize animal. Johnny dismounted, cut up his fine leather saddle, fashioned crude protective shoes for Oddfellow and continued on to the Ranch.

Paniolo means a gift for horsemanship. Back in 1906, Ikua Purdy and Archie Kaaua entered the Frontier Days competition in Cheyenne, Wyoming. In those days, the event was considered the Olympics of rodeo. Decked out in their vaquero finery--and astride unfamiliar mounts--the newcomers went head-to-head in steer roping with the best cowboys in the country. When the dust had settled, they had finished one-two in record time, Purdy then Kaaua,

before an electrified crowd. It was an unequalled feat that put the Hawaiian cowboy on the rodeo map.

The exploits of the old paniolos are legion. Theirs is a proud tradition that continues after nearly two centuries. And despite modern advances in the science of ranching, today's paniolos are still the backbone of Parker Ranch. They are equally at home tracking cattle on the far slopes of Mauna Kea, branding calves on the broad Waimea range, or running a rodeo in the town of Kamuela.

The tradition of the paniolo predates even those early vaqueros. Cattle were first introduced to the Islands in 1793 by Englishman George Vancouver. The sea captain

delivered five cows from California to King Kamehameha that year and two more cows and three bulls the following year. To protect these strange horned beasts, the king placed a kapu (taboo) on them punishable by death. In only a few years, thousands of cattle were running wild in the foothills of the island's great volcanoes.

So menacing were these feral animals that a new element of danger was introduced on the plains. Travelers and residents were gored from time to time by the bulls' rapier-sharp horns. Many were injured, some were killed. It would take good horses--and good men-- to control the cattle and begin tapping some promising new markets: beef, tallow and hides. The first of

the good men was John Palmer Parker.

The horses had come earlier. Ten years after Vancouver's arrival, another British sea captain, Richard Cleveland, delivered a mare and her foal to the local chief at Kawaihae. Other imported horses followed on their heels and soon, herds of wild mustangs were running as free as the cattle. The Hawaiians called the horse li'o, "wild-eyed."

Bullock hunting took off in the 1820s, as Parker and a growing number of frontiersmen stalked the animals through the mountains and valleys of west and central

Opposite page, far left: Brood mare band; right: Paniolo work saddles. Left: Historic shipping of cattle in early days. Above: Cattle are led into surf, then hoisted aboard vessel for transport to inter-island markets in Honolulu.

Hawaii. The beef was cut and salted on the spot and carried back to Kawaihae for barter with whaling ships or with merchantmen taking on loads of sandalwood. Although the fragrant wood had been the island's economic mainstay, depletion of the sandalwood forests was coming fast. Beef and its by-products represented a lucrative new commodity for filling that gap.

Still working under his royal commission, John Parker was a pioneer in the new industry. But it was clear to king and cattlemen alike that more sophisticated methods were necessary.

Espanol!

In 1832, Kamehameha III sent to California for vaqueros, accomplished horsemen to show Hawaiians the ropes. The first three to arrive--Louzeida, Ramon and Kossuth--became instant celebrities. Islanders were fascinated by these dashing Mexicans with their wide-brimmed sombreros, bright bandannas, slashed leggings and low-heeled boots. These malihini (newcomers) tied sharp knives to their right legs, trimmed their boots with jangling spurs, carried coiled lassos of rawhide, and rode beautifully stamped, hand-sewn saddles tied over colorful woolen blankets. They strummed ornate guitars, which would later inspire the ukulele, that symbol of the Islands.

The vaqueros were patient teachers, the Hawaiians eager learners. But while the Mexicans could impart what they knew about horsemanship and cattle roping, some things had to be learned on the job. The far-ranging island cattle, for instance, were wilder than any the vaqueros had encountered on the mainland. And the steep mountains, fields of sharp lava and thick tangles of mamane and mesquite provided greater challenges than any open range.

For the fledgling paniolo, the first order of business was catching and breaking one of the wild mustangs. These small, wild horses were tougher to tame and work than the finer mounts which Parker and others would import later. The Hawaiians also had to learn how to tan leather with tree bark, how to

43

Left: Kole Perreira, water dept. Opposite page, near left: Brocky Joaquin, Paniolo. Middle: Billy Andrade, Godfrey Kainoa, Dougie Cox getting ready for branding. Far right: Truck Driver, Leonard Case.

braid a lariat from rawhide or horsehair and how to build the tough Mexican-style saddles.

To fashion his lariat--the kaula ili--the paniolo scraped a choice hide and cut it into narrow strips. These were then softened and oiled in fat and braided into a tough, sinewy rope which was sometimes more than a hundred feet long. Shorter lassos were used for working the forests and ravines, longer for open country. Much later, of course, the rawhide gave way to the hemp and synthetic fabrics used today.

The early paniolo saddles used no tacks or nails, but were all planed and sewn by hand. Sturdy neleau wood was often used for the frame, pegs and okuma (pommel). Some of the paniolos added extra layers of leather for extra padding or ornamentation. Others, particularly those who swam cattle out to the longboats, opted for more spartan versions.

Once outfitted for the wilderness, the paniolos confronted the cattle. More often than not, they sought bulls, with their larger, higher-quality hides. Sometimes they roamed together in herds;

Paniolo Language

STARTING OFF THE DAY--BASICS

Hui hou	Run away (applied to cattle); to meet again (pau hana)
Ili o	Dog
Kakahiaka no	Early morning: an acknowledgement of the hour
Kau ka lio	Ride horse; used as a command for the paniolos to mount up and begin work
Lahai	Take the outside: a direction to the paniolos driving the cattle
Lio	Horse
Ma lalo	Take the under: a direction to the paniolos driving the cattle
Ma waena	Take the center: a direction to the paniolos driving the cattle
Oni	Time to move out, to start work
Pipi	Cattle
Waha	Make noise to keep the cattle moving

SEPARATION OF CATTLE

Alu	Let go; slack
Awaipuu	Lump jaw
Hemo ka puka	Open the gate

44

Hookawale	Separate cattle; put off to the side
Kanaha	Sore leg
Keiki/Kamalii	Calves
Ku puka paa	You watch the gate: command used while separating cattle
Kukue	One leg crooked
Kumulau	Cow
Laho	Bull
Laho ole	Steer
Likelike	Crippled
Luahine	Old cow
Mahape	The last
Maka ena	Sore eye
Maka ilo	Cancer eye
Makehewa	A waste of time
Mamua	The first
Mawaena	The middle
Ohi	Young heifer
Oki	To cut out the cattle while separating
Pani ka puka	Close the gate
Pau loa	All
Wawahi	Separate cattle

BRANDING--KUNIPIPI

Hana ka ahi	Get the branding stove ready
Hana ka laau	Get the medicine (wormers) ready
Ho hai kaula	Ropers to pull calves to the fire to be branded
Ku hi	Knock down men
Kui	Injections
Kuni	Brand

Laho	Male: this is called out loud so everyone will do their jobs faster
Oki hau	De-horn
Oki laho	Castrate
Wahine	Female: this is called out loud so everyone will do their jobs faster

GENERAL COMMANDS

Ahai ka paa	Follow along the fence line
Ahai ma mua	Follow the front
Alu alu ma mua	Chase the front
Awiwi	Hurry up; move faster
Eno	Pay attention when cattle is being called (slang)
Hana paa	Fix fence
Helu	Count
Hiki ole	Tired; overheated: used to apply to cattle, horses or paniolos
Hokuu	Let go; let the cattle go
Kahea	To call for identification of the cattle
Kani ka o	Stay in line: yelled to the paniolos when driving cattle over a large area
Ku ka laina	Hold the line: while lining up to separate the cattle, or hold at an entrance or water trough
Ku malia	Stand still: used to calm down the animals
Lio hou	Young horse
Makule	Old cow, bull or horse
Malia malia	Go slow and easy
Nana aina	Check paddocks
Nana pipi	Check cattle

Nana pono	Look good: do not miss any cattlemen bringing cattle together to drive
Nani wai	Check water
Nee imua	Move up front: said to other paniolos
Noho ma hape	Stay behind
Noho malia	Sit still: used to calm down the animals
Oleio	To talk, speak
Paa hou	Hold again
Paa ka laina	Come inside: used while lining up to separate the cattle, or hold them at an entrance or water trough
Paa ka ma ka mua	Hold the front: said when driving cattle
Paa ma hapo	Hold the rear: said when driving cattle
Paeke	Corral
Pili paa	To hold the cattle along the fence line
Weho	Leave along; leave behind: used to refer to cattle

COLORS OF LIVESTOCK

Apuai	Mouse brown
Ele ele	Black
Kalakoa	Black/white, red/white, brown/white
Keokeo	White
Mo o	Brindle
Nika	Black
Puakea	Light orange; yellowish
Ula ula	Red

other times they lurked in the brush, waiting to charge. Once the animal was flushed into a clearing, free of entangling vines or branches, the lasso had to be twirled and tossed with perfect precision. The lassoed bull was then pulled up short when the other end was wrapped quickly around the okuma--which was strained nearly to the breaking point.

Then came the moment of truth. If the enraged bull charged, both horse and rider could be maimed or killed. But if he continued to buck and lunge at the end of the lariat, the paniolo could work his way to a nearby tree and wrap the rope around it. With the bull thus securely fastened, the cowboy could ride off in search of others. In this way, he could catch a half-dozen or more in a single long, dangerous day.

The following morning, the paniolos returned to the clearing with a tame bull in tow and tied the two together. Inevitably, the domesticated animal had a calming effect on the wild one, and later in the day, the two could be led together back to the pens at Ranch headquarters. This natural taming effect was also employed on a broader scale. Paniolos might drive a domesticated herd into an area frequented by wild cattle, allow them to mingle, then drive them all back to the pens together.

Another task was required when it came time to ship cattle to market in Honolulu and on other islands. This was hoau, moving the animals through the shorebreak to

Opposite page: working cattle at Aalii I corral in Waikii section of Mauna Kea division. Above: paniolos branding calves, Kohala division. Right: Brocky Joaquin shoeing a horse.

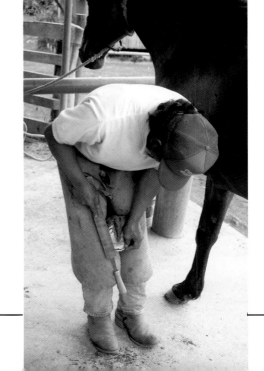

→

→

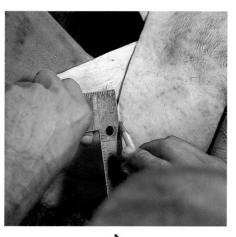

→

→

Saddle maker: Kalei Lindsey.
Saddle-making: photos from left to right,
starting at top: The first photo shows the
rawhide wrapped around the okumu
(pommel), ready to be trimmed and cut
into strips for braiding. The following
photos show the saddle-maker measuring
and cutting the awe-awe, the rawhide piece
which wraps around the okumu and braids
to the front cinch rings. The braids will
attach to the front cinch rings of the
finished saddle. (Second row, third from
right): The leather strip coming from
under the skirt will be cut into strips and
braided to form the last braid on this side
of the awe-awe. The final photos show the
completed left side of the awe-awe and an
underpiece being cut from skirting leather
for the rest of the saddle.

the waiting steamers. A day of hoau started just after midnight, when the paniolos rolled out of their bunks and rode to the pad-

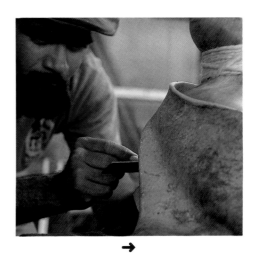

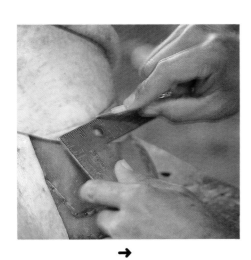

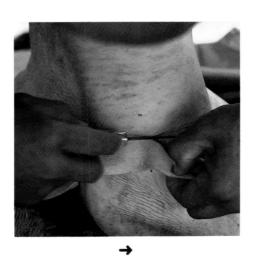

docks to pick up the shipment. This newly gathered herd was then driven down to the beach at Kawaihae before dawn, avoiding the cattle weight loss that came from driving in the hot sun. Here in the dusty beach hamlet--with its crude shacks and a handful of primitive government buildings-- the best riders and best horses began escorting the panicky cattle to the inter-island steamer lying in the harbor.

Leading it with his rope, the mounted paniolo would force a steer into the water and through

the surf. Horse and steer swam side-by-side out to a dinghy just offshore. Here, the cattle were lashed to the sides--up to a half-dozen on each side. Ropes tied around snout and ears held the animal's head above water, and the dinghy was then pulled by hand-line out to the inter-island steamer: the Hornet or the Humuula, the Bee or the Hawaii. Once alongside the ship, the steer was untied and hoisted aboard by a winch with a sling which was wrapped under its belly. On deck, the cattle's horns were lashed to the railings to prevent jostling and injury.

Danger was everywhere during the hoau operation--and not just from the frightened cattle. Sharks often trolled the waters off Kawaihae in search of an easy meal. And on windy days when seas were high, shipping cattle in this manner was many times more difficult. Nevertheless, hoau would continue as a common practice well into the twentieth century--when an eighty-thousand-dollar-wharf was finally completed at Kawaihae.

The early paniolos had many other responsibilities, and not all of them were quite so dangerous. He groomed and cared for his horses, spruced up his saddle and tack, chopped wood, mended fences and tended to a myriad of other chores. But John Parker was a fair employer, they knew, who would always treat them right. And each day brought new adventure on the open range of Waimea or the pristine slopes of Mauna Kea--a breathtaking world of wide blue skies and gentle mists. Living and working in perfect harmony with this magnificent land, the paniolo would trade his rigorous life for no other.

The New Breed

These days, modern technology has helped eliminate much of the danger and drudgery of paniolo life. Parker Ranch's 55,000 head of cattle are domesticated livestock, much easier to track and control than their wild ancestors. Today, cattle are dehorned and shipped to market in large container ships moored at modern wharf facilities. No longer are they herded to shore; rather they are driven to the docks in large trucks and handled with kid gloves--all in the interest of protecting the beef. Out on the range, much of the patrolling can be done in quick, dependable four-wheel-drive vehicles.

But being a paniolo can still be risky business. Much of the Ranch's more remote acreage is only accessible to a good rider on a well-trained mount. And there are plenty of tough, dusty jobs which

rely almost solely on manpower: branding, tagging, castration of young bulls. Now more than ever, the paniolo is the key to the successful running of Parker Ranch.

Today, some three dozen skilled horsemen can claim this term of distinction. A few have worked the range since the days when Alfred Carter's son, Hartwell, managed the Ranch. There is Dan Kaniho, whose father, Willie, retired in 1966 after fifty years as a paniolo. When Willie was born in 1894, his own father worked on the Ranch at Humuula. Willie was later made a foreman to replace paniolo Junichi Ishuzu, who was killed in a flash flood after he and his horse were caught in a torrent.

Also a paniolo today is Charlie Kimura, son of the legendary Yutaka Kimura. In nearly a half-century with the Ranch, this child of a poor Japanese immigrant family grew to become one of the finest

Parker Ranch paniolos at the Waiemi section in the Mauna Kea division, ready for the day's work.

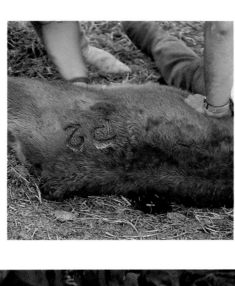

paniolos ever under the tutelage of Alfred Carter.

Flushing reluctant cattle from the bush. Swimming panicky animals out to sea. Fixing a fence in a tropical storm. Whatever the task, the paniolo was there. Today, though parts of his job have given way to modern technology, the Hawaiian cowboy still rides herd. It's the paniolo, as always, who makes Hawaii's cattle kingdom work.

53

Opposite page: paniolos Donnie DeSilva (center) and Andrew Kawai (background), rounding up a stray during a cattle drive. Above: Paniolos branding in the Kohala division.

CHAPTER III

The Ranch Today

A Day in the Life

Morning at Parker Ranch: a fine dew blankets the meadows, and cattle mill and moan beneath skies as clear as a paniolo's song. Later, fast-creeping clouds will build great vaults in the eastern sky and obscure the mountain peaks that define the Ranch.

But for now, the eye can trace the old lava flows that etch still-active Mauna Loa, count the snow-white observatories atop Mauna Kea, and see the high forests cloaking the wind-sculpted Kohala Mountains. In the distance to the west, Maui's Haleakala soars ten thousand feet through the ocean mists.

Morning comes early at the Ranch, perhaps earliest of all for the paniolo, who gulps black coffee and gobbles breakfast at one of the remote outback stations, then rides out to tend his cattle or mend his fences before the midday heat sets in. The town of Kamuela comes alive, too, as residents gather at

Auntie Alice's or the Paniolo Country Inn to greet the new day. At Ranch Headquarters nearby, administrators are gearing up the machinery that powers Parker Ranch.

A dozing cowtown only a century ago, Kamuela today hums and bustles with the vitality of small-town America. General stores like the venerable Hayashi's still offer the staples of Ranch life, from poi to parasols, tennis shoes to tire irons. Expert craftsmen sell fine leather items, and the Kamuela Hat Company displays its felt

Stetsons and western straw hats. But a growing population of newcomers–many from Oahu and the mainland–has prompted the opening of new boutiques, art galleries and other upscale establishments. Because the area is also a bedroom community for the Kohala Coast resorts, morning brings the Kamuela commute, as the work force heads down the mountain toward the posh hotels and award-winning golf courses.

As day progresses, a steady stream of visitors quickens the pace of life in Kamuela. Arriving from Kohala and Kona, or from Hilo to

the east, they pose for photos by the rustic corrals, poke through the Parker Ranch Store for logo items or browse the shopping centers for maps and souvenirs. Rental cars and sporty four-wheel-drives round the circular drive at Puuopelu or stop for lunch at Hale Kea, the restored former home of Alfred Wellington Carter and other Ranch managers.

Afternoons at the center of town, picturesque Waimea Park hosts baseball and soccer games for the children of Kamuela, who attend Waimea School and Honokaa High–or the town's two excellent prep schools, Parker School and Hawaii Preparatory Academy.

Thanks to the area's unique mix of Ranch people, new residents and visitors, good restaurants abound, and the small town has a big fol-

Preceding pages 54–55, inset: Blue Coleman, superintendent of Mauna Kea division, roping calves at branding time. A view of a tree plot at Airport Paddock, in the Waiemi section of the Mana division some years ago. Opposite page: Paniolo Kale Stevens sorting cattle in the Makahalau section of the Mana division some years ago. Above, left: Parker Ranch Shopping Center in the Kamuela section. Right: The old sheep station in the Humuula section.

lowing among island gourmets. Some of the best chefs in the country, including a few from the Kohala hotels, have hung out their shingles in Kamuela. The fine dining ranges from savory surf-and-turf to the latest in Hawaii regional cuisine–that exotic blend of flavors from the Pacific Rim, Europe and Asia.

On special nights, evening in Kamuela might also include a world-class performance at the Kahilu Theatre. The Big Island's only true center for the performing arts, Richard Smart's pride and joy stages everything from Gershwin to Wagner, from ballet to Broadway. On really special nights, Smart himself might have headlined a Lerner and Loewe musical or a Noel Coward revue. Managing director of the theatre is Virginia Pfaff, formerly with the famed Wolf Trap facility near Washington, D.C.

But after the last curtain call at the Kahilu Theatre, when a fat tropical moon hangs high over Mauna Kea, Kamuela is a cowtown once again. Slumbering on its Big Island plateau, Kamuela by night, at least, seems little changed from the pioneering days of John Palmer Parker.

58

Above: A rehearsal in progress at the Kahilu Theater. Opposite page: another breathtaking sunset viewed from the Kohala mountains.

A Working Ranch

The Ranch itself, of course, has changed with the times.

Sometimes it has changed ahead of them. Today Parker Ranch enjoys a place in the forefront of the cattle industry. That's partly because its unique mid-Pacific location has prompted bold steps and creative innovations.

For all its historical drama and eye-popping beauty, the Ranch is first and foremost a cattle producer. Its 55,000 head produce USDA choice beef marketed in the U.S. and Canada. It's the third largest herd in the U.S., after those at the King Ranch in Texas and the Deseret Ranch in Florida.

The cattle are a crossbreed of Angus, Brangus and polled (hornless) Hereford. At one time, under Alfred Wellington Carter, Parker Ranch boasted the largest purebred Hereford herd in the country. But in recent years, the three breeds have been combined to produce an animal perfectly suited to the area's climate and range conditions. Three separate purebred herds of four hundred females each are maintained to produce bulls for this breeding program. In addition, cows are bred with bull semen and with herd sires imported from the mainland, to constantly improve the stock.

The Ranch's 20,000 cows are the core of cattle production. The rest of the herd is made up of replacement heifers, bulls and calves. In the Big Island's sub-

Opposite page: Hereford cows in the Mauna Kea division. Above: Sorting calves to be given shots.

Below: Some Hereford cows of years past. Opposite page: A typical commercial Brangus breeding bull on Parker Ranch.(Makahalau station in background.)

tropical climate, they graze year-round in four separate cattle divisions. These are the Kohala division, the Ranch's leeward reaches; the Mana division, the great plain between Kamuela and Mauna Kea; the Mauna Kea division, higher on the Mauna Kea volcano's slope; and the Keamuku/Humuula division, on Mauna Kea's southern and eastern flanks. Herds can range in size from two hundred head of cattle to fifteen hundred or even more, depending upon pasture size.

In the spring and fall, calves are branded with Parker Ranch's distinctive "P" and inoculated against blackleg, a bacterial disease. Young males are desexed at this time. Thereafter, at six months of age, the calves are weaned from their mothers. The calves are then trucked to one of two intensive grazing areas in Kohala or Mana near Kamuela where they are settled and staged for their next journey.

Then begins the animals' longest journey. A generation ago, they were shipped by barge from Kawaihae for further fattening at the Ranch's Hawaii Meat Co. feed-

64

Above: Cows and calves in a corral in the Waikii section, Mauna Kea division. Opposite page: Paniolos vaccinating and processing calves for export.

lot outside Honolulu. That facility was also used by dozens of other Hawaii ranchers. But with the high cost of importing mainland grain, finishing cattle in the Islands was an expensive proposition indeed. Management began seeking other avenues to market and began phasing out the Oahu feedlot.

In 1990, Parker Ranch began shipping its cattle directly to the mainland for fattening and finishing. At the docks at Kawaihae they are loaded into massive cargo ships built expressly for the purpose. These are the vessels of the Corral Line, registered in Denmark. Corral runs fifteen such ships, including the one most often used

65

by the Ranch, the *Philomena Purcell*. It's the biggest in the fleet, and it can carry more than two thousand of the five-hundred-pound cattle.

The animals destined for Canadian consumption arrive in Vancouver after an air-cooled, eight-day voyage, and spend several months grazing on grass until they weigh nine hundred pounds. From there, they are trucked to feedlots in the Calgary area, where they are fattened for a hundred days, then slaughtered at twelve hundred pounds and marketed primarily in eastern Canada. All told, the Ranch produces more than ten million pounds of beef each year.

But Parker Ranch beef begins on the range, where the paniolos share the responsibility of raising them right. Typically, each cowboy has some fifteen hundred head of cattle in his charge. To help him in the task, he is given eight fine horses which he keeps shod and maintained. His mounts are kept in stables at the paniolo's assigned division. When he retires, his favorite one is his to keep.

The horses of Parker Ranch are second to none. A combination of thoroughbred and quarterhorse, they are bred for speed and utility

Opposite page: the Philomena Purcell of the Corral Line loading a shipment of cattle for export to Canada. Above: Corral Line is Danish registry; George Liana, a trucker, is loading calves on truck for export; and a small spectator, a green turtle, takes it all in.

67

Clockwise from top: Paniolo Buddy Gomes on a young horse; Brocky Joaquin assisting on a Mauna Kea cattle drive; Brood mares and foals in Makahalau section of Mana division. Opposite page, clockwise from top left: Brood mares and foals, also from Makahalau section; Sonny Keakealani, foreman of the Makahalau section, closes a corral gate; Blue Coleman, superintendent for Mauna Kea division, leads a horse to work.

in cutting calves, roping and other activities. There are four hundred of them at the Ranch–three hundred work horses and another one hundred brood mares and yearlings. The breeding program is recognized in the industry as one of the best anywhere, with forty-eight mares bred to four stallions each year.

Water supply, of course, is critical to such a sprawling operation. Each day, Parker Ranch drinks in a whopping 400,000 gallons. This is runoff from the Kohala Mountains, most of it captured by damming a Kohala stream. From there, it is then piped by gravity to most of the acreage, and pumped

68

Oposite page: PaAalii Reservoir, Waikii section, Mauna Kea division, holds 30 million gallons of water for cattle. It is one of the five major reservoirs on the ranch. There are also at least 100 small ones. Right: Haru Honma, foreman for the garage; Truckers ready to roll out; Mechanic Charlie Pahio; Trucking department foreman, Arthur Akau.

up to its higher reaches. Elsewhere on the Ranch, newly drilled wells provide artesian water for community consumption.

Water management decisions–and other important calls–are made primarily at Ranch Headquarters in the heart of Kamuela. This is where the administrative staff maintains the operational nerve center. The office employees are part of the Ranch's total payroll of nearly 120 people–paniolos, planners, truck drivers, secretaries, fence crew, shopping center maintenance workers and others.

Employee turnover is low at Parker Ranch, and not just because of family tradition and the working environment. Paniolos and others enjoy an excellent compensation package, including housing. Employees who want to own their own homes can buy an inexpensive Ranch lot, then build with low-interest construction financing. If they opt to purchase elsewhere, they receive a housing allowance to make up for the lost benefits.

In 1970, Richard Smart launched a profit-sharing plan. There are ranch-style benefits, too. Employees can graze two horses each on company land. And every worker receives five pounds of beef each week; married employees get ten.

71

Above: The Parker Ranch Christmas tree at the entry to Puuopelu stands over 100 feet tall, and each winter is adorned with Christmas lights. Opposite page: Scenes from the annual 4th of July races, with the American flag flanked by the state of Hawaii flag. Paniolo legend Willie Kaniho rides in an early 4th of July celebration.

One of the most important benefits of Ranch employment is the community spirit–the sense of being part of the family. In the fall, management stages the Parker Ranch Ho'oponopono at the Kahilu Theatre. Once called the Animal Health Conference, this annual event has grown into a general update on operations, with an eye on both the year ahead and the long-term future.

Come Christmas, all employees attend the State of the Ranch Meeting at Kahilu Town Hall, which focuses on the year just past. That evening, the workers and their families celebrate the season with a gala Christmas party, also held at Town Hall. At Puuopelu, the lone one hundred-fifty-foot pine tree by the estate's front drive is decorated and lit, a traditional beacon in the pasture-land. It's one of Parker Ranch's most festive occasions.

The other big event happens the morning of the Fourth of July. The Parker Ranch Rodeo and Horse Races are an annual

Left: The annual Fourth of July horse races and rodeo have been going on for approximately 35 years at the Ranch. It's a chance for the hardworking paniolos to show the community and visitors alike their unique talents. Below: Frank Hess and Gary Rapozo, marketing cattle superintendent. Retirees Joe Cordiero, Jiro Yamaguchi, and Martin Purdy wait for their event.

74

institution on the Big Island, with paniolos and others showing their skills on horseback. There's thoroughbred racing, plenty of island music and several rodeo events: team penning, double mugging, "wild" cow milking and team roping.

For visitors, there's no better time to see the paniolos in action. But this day, there's something more. For the Fourth of July is also a window on Ranch life—a close-up look at an unusual Hawaiian community that works and plays together as it has for many generations.

Top, left to right: The Honorable Kalani Schuttee, County Councilman, enjoys the races; Craig Pasqual-paniolo/participant; Godfrey Kainoa and Mark Yamaguchi getting rid of butterflies before event.

CHAPTER IV

A Tale of Two Homes

Hill of Hiding

Legend has it that Puuopelu was named during an historic Hawaiian battle. At the height of hostilities, Big Islanders say, a princess sought refuge in the area. Puu means "hill," and pelu means "doubled up" or "hiding."

Puuopelu: "hill of hiding." Another version holds that Puuopelu means "folding hills."

In more recent times, this place of lore and legend has provided a refuge of sorts for the owners of Parker Ranch. For more than a century, their sprawling estate has stood here overlooking the Waimea plain. Once it was home to John Palmer Parker II, first-born son of the Ranch patriarch. Most recently it was the address of Richard Palmer Smart, who represented the sixth generation of the Big Island line.

Today's Puuopelu is open to the public, allowing visitors a fascinat-

78

Preceding pages 76–77: The entrance to Puuopelu; with Mana Hale in its modern location, to the right. (inset) Richard Smart with one of the Ranch stallions.
Above: Mana Hale at its modern site.
Right: Mana Hale at its original site.
Opposite page: original Parker bed with a Hawaiian quilt.

ing look at the Parkers. Flanking a circular drive at the end of a tree-lined entry road, the handsome estate features expansive, impeccably furnished French Provincial interiors, manicured gardens and one of the finest Impressionist art collections anywhere.

Also on the grounds of Puuopelu is Mana Hale, the nineteenth-century patriarchal home. In 1977, much of the old house was brought down off the slopes of Mauna Kea and rebuilt on this spot board-for-board. Inside the clapboard building, original furniture and old photos illustrate life on the Ranch as it was in the mid-nineteenth century.

79

The Parker Homes:
Puuopelu and Mana Hale

Mana Hale

The story of Puuopelu goes back to those early years, when most of the family still lived together at Mana, on the upslope land first sold to John Palmer Parker for a token ten dollars. The dwelling echoed John Parker's childhood memories of New England–a simple home with a steep slate roof and multi-paned windows. But inside, the walls, floors and ceilings were fashioned from rich Hawaiian koa wood, and mattresses were stuffed with the springy pulu from hapuu ferns. This was Mana Hale, "house of the spirit," a handsome frontier address that would welcome travelers to Waimea for generations.

In no time, this cheerful residence on the mountainside became a welcome stop for cross-island travelers. John Parker held court with a mix of Christian and Polynesian customs. Every Sunday, for instance, a church service was held, with all hymns sung in Hawaiian. Mana Hale had no fireplace, but when the temperature dipped in the evenings, a large washtub filled with glowing charcoal was brought into the living room. The Parkers would warm themselves by it, burn sandalwood in it to scent the room, and roast peanuts plucked from their garden.

A highlight of an evening at Mana Hale was the entertainment. For many years, John Parker had learned the ways of the Hawaiians. Dressed in a malo (loincloth), he would recite ancient chants, telling stories and tracing genealogy. Parker had learned oli (chanting) from one of Hawaii's best–his own brother-in-law Kapuaa. Trained in the court of Kamehameha I, Kapuaa also lived at Mana and could hold family and visitors spellbound with his great vocal range and enchanting tales.

As his two sons grew and married, John built them each their own accommodations at Mana. When the old cattleman died in 1868, he left just two male heirs: John II and his grandson Sam, the only surviving son of the late Ebenezer. For awhile, they lived side-by-side–John and his Hanai, and Sam with his wife, Panana.

But this arrangement quickly brought conflict between uncle and nephew because of their differ-ent lifestyles. Sam and his wife had begun to entertain lavishly shortly after their marriage, and Sam's reputation for hospitality increased the fame of Mana Hale.

In 1879, John elected to move both his own home and Ranch operations closer to the village of Waimea. An Englishman named Notley had built a fine home just outside town on a scenic knoll called Puuopelu. Notley was leaving Waimea for the booming sugar business on the Hamakua Coast, and John bought the estate, with its tall trees, grassy meadows and small lake next to the house.

Puuopelu has been in the family ever since. After John II passed away in 1891, it was the residence of his nephew John Parker III, who died at the age of nineteen. After that, it became a second home for John III's widow Elizabeth, or Aunt Tootsie, as she was called, and their daughter, Thelma. They stayed at Puuopelu each summer, when they left San Francisco for Hawaii. In 1910, they added a second increment, including a larger living room and a kitchen wing.

After Thelma died, Elizabeth kept the same living arrangement

Puuopelu

for herself and Thelma's son, Richard Smart. The matronly Elizabeth and young Richard lived in San Francisco for the majority of the year, yet every summer they returned to Puuopelu.

In 1948, five years after Elizabeth died, Smart created a dining room at Puuopelu by splitting the kitchen wing in half. In 1960, when he returned to Hawaii after his twenty-five-year show business career, Puuopelu became his primary Big Island residence. Under his guidance, the estate was spruced up inside and out. The wooden living room area was replaced with a more durable structure of concrete and steel. An extensive rose garden and other new plantings were added. And Smart began hanging his superb collection of French impressionist paintings and other fine art.

Before long, Puuopelu had been restored to its former sparkle. A gracious host and entertainer, Richard Smart invited a steady stream of guests to his country estate. Not since the days of Sam Parker had Kamuela seen such gala parties. There were picnics and other functions for Ranch employees. There were elaborate costume balls and theme parties, with guests flying in from Honolulu and the mainland to join the festivities. At Smart's Black and White Ball, for instance, partygoers wore only black and white, and old Hollywood celebrity photos were mounted to cover the colorful paintings hanging throughout Puuopelu.

Visiting Puuopelu

Today, the private quarters are closed during the regular hours when the home is open to the public. Visitors enter through large double doors into a great, high-ceilinged living room filled with antiques and objets d'art. The dining room, library, bedrooms and smaller sitting rooms are beautifully filled with priceless art and furnishings. One, the Venetian Room, shows Smart's love of Italy, particularly Venice. Bedrooms boast hand-carved koa beds covered with lush Hawaiian quilts. Everywhere are European heirloom furniture, crystal chandeliers and delicate figurines.

It was Richard Smart who in 1987 directed the reconstruction of Mana Hale just steps from Puuopelu's front door. Here, the historic home is easily accessible to visitors, who can peruse the old photos and documents on display and tread the same floorboards where John Parker chanted for his guests.

Portraits of Parkers adorn the walls: stern John, dashing Sam, lovely Thelma. King David Kalakaua is pictured, lounging about with his friend Sam Parker, and old-time paniolos pose on the range. Glass cases protect well-preserved old letters, like the one from John Parker's mother sent from Massachusetts in 1819, or the one written by Princess Kaiulani.

On the grounds surrounding the two homes, visitors can stroll through the manicured gardens overlooking the pond and charming pumphouse, admire the wide variety of blooms in the rose garden, or gaze up at the immense pine that serves as the Ranch's Christmas tree. From this scenic setting, the Waimea plain sweeps off in every direction to the far reaches of Parker Ranch.

81

The Art of Puuopelu: The Richard Smart Collection

82

Above: statue by John Van Nost, Diana, *1770; Murano glass chandelier. Opposite page: living room at Puuopelu.*

For all its history and heritage, Puuopelu's most striking attraction is its bounty of fine art. The collection includes more than one hundred paintings, plates, vases and works of sculpture.

Richard Smart began collecting art in 1951, when he headlined at the famed Lido night club in Paris. Because foreigners weren't allowed to take their newly earned francs out of France, Smart bought several paintings and shipped his earnings back to Hawaii in the form of art. These first acquisitions were examples of the Impressionist school which he had long admired. In later years, he added many more paintings during his annual trips to London and the Continent. Other works have been acquired from galleries and dealers in the U.S.

If Smart's collection has any one overall theme, it is the great outdoors. At Puuopelu, portraits and still lifes are few and far between. The pastoral beauty of many of the paintings, in fact, echoes the gentle rural setting outside. The dozens of paintings are augmented by exquisite objets, from a collection of nineteenth-century plates to priceless vases from the Ming dynasty (1368-1644). Glass display cases hold the likes of antique Chinese vases, figurines of jade and amethyst, Peking glass carvings, a bronze head of Buddha from Thailand, and roof tiles from the Ch'ien Lung Reign (1736-1795). Other cases protect a nineteenth-century Meissen monkey orchestra from Germany, a Tang Dynasty (618-906) camel with rider, a Capot di Monte dinner service, and many other priceless collectibles.

On the walls hang canvasses by Degas and Renoir, Corot and Tissot. Many of them are scenes of Venice, Paris and the south of France. Island artists are here, too, with two works by Lloyd Sexton and portraits of Smart and his late friend Charles Gregory painted by Marilyn Sunderman.

The French Impressionist paintings represent the very best of the period. The oil by Pierre Auguste Renoir, for example, is "Tete de Femme," painted in 1878. Renoir was considered the old master of the impressionists, with his meticulous attention to form and color.

The work by Edgar Degas is "Le Village," an oil on canvas created at the very end of the nineteenth century. A maverick of the Impressionist movement, Degas specialized in scenes of daily

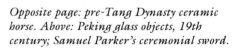

Opposite page: pre-Tang Dynasty ceramic horse. Above: Peking glass objects, 19th century; Samuel Parker's ceremonial sword.

French living: cafes and bistros, working people, ballet dancers, race track scenes.

Jean Corot is represented by "L'lle Heureuse" and "La Mare aux Vaches," both oils painted in the mid-nineteenth century. A French landscape and figure painter, Corot was greatly influenced by his studies in Germany and Italy.

In addition to its superb range of French Impressionists, the Smart collection includes American Impressionist works by Frederick Childe Hassam and Theodore Butler, as well as paintings by French Post-Impressionists, among them Henri Le Basque, Lucien Pissarro and Henri Martin. Together, the fine art at Puuopelu adds a stunning extra dimension to this historic estate on the plains of Parker Ranch.

*Opposite page: Pierre Montezin (1874-
1946), La Moisson, undated. Right:
Dresden chocolate set. Above: Jean Corot
(1796-1875), L'lle Heureuse, undated.
Left: Peking glass bowl, 19th century.*

88

Opposite page, right: Delos Palmer, Portrait
of Thelma Parker Palmer, 1950; below:
William James, Basino de San Marco,
1761–1771. Above: Chinese jade sculpture
of young woman, attendant and deer;
Right: Henri Martin (1860–1952),
Landscape, undated.

89

Above: Maurice De Vlaminck (1876–1958), Le Champ de Blu, *undated; right: Maurice Utrillo (1883–1955),* Street Scene in Poissy, France, *1929. Opposite page: Lloyd Sexton (c. 1920–1991),* Holo Holo Ku, *undated.*

90

CHAPTER V

The Parker Legacy

Kamuela at the Crossroads

John Palmer Parker would not recognize the place. With its bustling shopping centers, fine schools and modern medical facilities, the town of Kamuela is a far cry from the dusty cowtown he helped create. The cattle that roamed the streets back then have given way to four-wheel-drives and sightseers' rental cars. The weathered general stores have been replaced by fast food outlets and filling stations.

Till now, growth in the Waimea area has come in fairly orderly fashion. But economic and demographic factors are tugging harder than ever at the town limits. In recent years, more and more outsiders–particularly from Oahu and the mainland–have discovered the area's rustic charm and bracing climate. Designer homes are popping up on ocean-view lots and the forested knolls around Kamuela.

How will the area's popularity affect roads, water supply and other infrastructure? What impact will it have on housing, health care and the environment? How will future generations perceive their upcountry home?

To answer these questions–and to ensure that Waimea's growth doesn't run rampant–Richard

Smart, before his death in 1992, and Ranch planners developed a master plan for the lands adjacent to the town center. Working with designers, architects, environmentalists, archaeologists and other specialists, they built a framework for the future called Parker Ranch 2020.

Naturally, this blueprint for a twenty-first century Waimea encourages growth that is compatible with the area's rural ambience. New commercial structures will be "ranch style," in design, scale and materials. The impact of cars and trucks will be minimized. Precious views toward Mauna Kea, Mauna Loa, the Kohala Mountains and the surrounding foothills will be preserved. An integrated system of equestrian trails, bike paths and hiking trails will link key public facilities with Waimea's great outdoors.

Parker Ranch 2020 covers three primary areas. Largest of these, and the focal point of the plan, is 480 acres at the town center. "Downtown" Kamuela will be the hub of Waimea's social, cultural, educational and commercial activi-

ties–for shopping, dining, doing business or attending world-class performances at the Kahilu Theatre. Curving, tree-lined streets will guide residents and visitors past new medical and police facilities, an expanded Parker Ranch Shopping Center, a senior citizens' center, a relocated Parker School and an expanded Waimea School. A brand new Ranch headquarters will be built, and parks and other open space will abound.

The plan's second major development is a light industrial and high-tech park west of the Waimea-Kohala Airport. Covering twenty-five acres and effectively screened by large trees and other landscaping, this facility will include traditional light industry, as well as astronomy support facilities for the observatories clustered at the top of Mauna Kea. The plan calls for large lots, limited access from the highway and careful development in small increments.

Also vital to Parker Ranch 2020 is a 190-acre parcel for more resi-

dential and agricultural lots to the west of town. Homes built on these lots will reflect the same rural character as those already in place.

Water exploration and development is critical to the area's growth. Accordingly, considerable funds have been earmarked for groundwater studies, and test wells have been drilled at several sites. As the Ranch works with State and Hawaii County water boards, it also coordinates with the respective government planning agencies for the rezoning and district changes necessary for individual projects to begin. Also consulted are the owners and operators of the beach resorts along the island's Kohala Coast, which have been heavily involved with their own long-range planning for years.

The detailed blueprint of Parker Ranch 2020 makes it easy to envision the Kamuela of the future. Careful, creative and far-sighted, it will benefit the area's increasingly cosmopolitan mix of residents and visitors, Ranch employees and others who make this country community their home.

Preceding pages 92–93: Parker Ranch offices in Kamuela; Parker Ranch Broiler, a popular restaurant. Above: This Parker Ranch poster, in its traditional woodcut style, recalls the spirit of the 19th century paniolos and Hawaii's cattle kingdom.

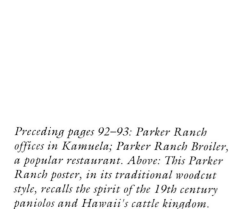

The Parker Ranch Team

The special legacy of Richard Smart and his forebears is now in the hands of these men, who have a rich understanding of the traditions of Parker Ranch. The Ranch trustees oversee the Parker Ranch Foundation Trust, a legacy that includes grants to local schools, medical facilities, and community cultural activities.

The trustees and management of Parker Ranch also have a very important responsibility, as the Ranch and the surrounding community face the challenge of the next century. Growth has to be balanced with reverence for the past. The people of the Ranch and the surrounding Waimea community recognize that need, and are planning their future accordingly—with the Parker Ranch 2020 master plan as a guide.

Their work reflects the unique spirit of Richard Smart, who loved his community and established the Parker Ranch Foundation Trust to keep alive the special relationship between a Hawaii country town and Hawaii's largest working cattle ranch.

Above (left to right): Warren J. Gunderson, managing trustee; Melvin B. Hewett, trustee; Robert L. Hind, III, livestock manager.

For his part, Richard Smart made it clear that the Ranch will remain a living, working entity. His two sons, Tony and Gilliard, both of whom once held management positions there, have chosen to pursue their own outside interests. Smart's heirs benefited from his personal estate.

To keep Parker Ranch intact after his death, Smart placed it in a charitable trust for the benefit of its valued employees and their families. This trust not only allows for continued company operations but also provides medical, educational and cultural benefits for the Kamuela community.

For the people of Parker Ranch, this future is a fitting one. Some of them are fourth-generation ranchers–whose fathers shipped cattle for Hartwell Carter, whose grandfathers mended fences for Alfred Carter, whose great-grandparents rode the range for John Parker II. Now this loyalty can be repaid.

The Parker Ranch saga has always been a people story, since that day in 1809 when a young seaman met a warrior king. Thanks to the Richard Smart Trust, this story will continue–an epic tale of proud paniolos and skilled ranchers in a unique Hawaiian home.

Guide to Parker Ranch

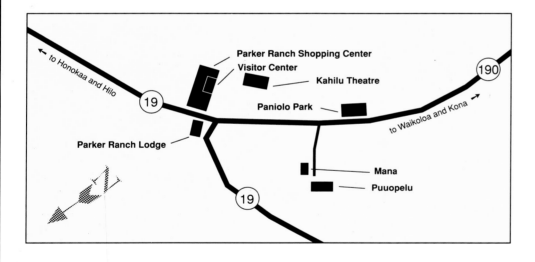

From the Big Island's Kona Coast, Kamuela–the heart of Parker Ranch–can be reached by driving north along the Queen Kaahumanu Highway, then east on Highway 19 from the coastal village of Kawaihae. Drive time is approximately one hour from Kona's main town, Kailua-Kona. From East Hawaii, Kamuela is a one-and-a-half hour drive from the island's county seat of Hilo, north on Highway 11. Several Big Island tour operators also offer bus and van tours that include Parker Ranch. There are major inter-island airports at both Kailua-Kona and Hilo.

Hotel and bed-and-breakfast accommodations are available in Kamuela, including the 21-room Parker Ranch Lodge in the center of town. Luxury hotels and resort condominiums are located along the leeward Kohala Coast, ten miles west of Kamuela.

Above: This map shows the location of the Parker Ranch historic homes, the Kahilu Theatre, and the visitor's center; Parker Ranch tour bus. Inside Back Cover: The entrance to the Parker Ranch shopping center; The Kahilu Theatre.
Inside back flap: The Parker Ranch store is a popular site for memorable gifts and souvenirs from a visit to the island of Hawaii and its cattle kingdom. Outside back flap: Gordon Lindsay, foreman of the fence crew.